GW00357389

for the one life we have

BRITISH HUMANIST ASSOCIATION

The British Humanist Association exists to promote Humanism and support and represent people who seek to live good lives without religious or superstitious beliefs.

In the same series by Jane Wynne Willson:

Funerals Without God: a practical guide to non-religious ceremonies (British Humanist Association 1989, second edition 1990, third edition 1992, fourth, extended edition 1995).

Sharing the Future: a practical guide to non-religious wedding/affirmation ceremonies (British Humanist Association 1988, second edition 1989, third edition 1994, fourth extended edition 1996, fifth edition 2005).

© British Humanist Association 1991, second edition 1995, third revised and enlarged edition March 1999, fourth edition 2002, fifth edition 2005.

All rights reserved.

Printed by RAP Spiderweb Ltd., Clowes Street, Hollinwood, Oldham OL9 7LY.
Cover printed on 100% post consumer recycled stock.
Internal pages printed on 75% post consumer recycled, chlorine free from sustainable resources.

ISBN 0901825166

Contents

Outline

Introduction   5

A ceremony that suits everyone   5

A unique ceremony   6

Where and when?   6

Supporting adults   7

A framework for the ceremony   8

Who should lead the ceremony?   8

Examples and ideas

Introducing the ceremony   10

Responsibilities and aspirations for your child   12

The formal naming   15

Appointing supporting adults   16

Involving more people in the ceremony   17

Special ways of marking the occasion   17

Ideas for poetry and prose readings   19

Using music   36

Two examples of complete ceremonies   37

About the BHA   43

Further reading   43

Acknowledgements   44

humanist baby namings

Introduction

Congratulations on your new child! Just like you, many parents are keen to mark the arrival of their new baby with a special occasion, which we call a naming ceremony. But in fact it means so much more than simply giving your child their name. The occasion is a celebration, with your family and friends around you, and it is a time when you can affirm your commitment to your child in front of those who mean most to you — a very special welcome.

Most families have some sort of party, and including a naming ceremony is a chance for you to make the day even more memorable.

A ceremony that suits everyone

Humanism is non-religious, and has no worship, fixed rituals, or dogmatic rules other than the desire that each of us should make the most of life, and try to benefit other people and the world while we're doing so.

A humanist baby naming, wedding, affirmation or funeral is inclusive. Our ceremonies are based on what we all have in common – our humanity and human values – and this transcends any religious beliefs that some of the people present may have.

Our ceremonies are chosen by many different families: two married or unmarried parents, single parents, adoptive parents, step-parents, parents who are of different religions or cultures, and lesbian or gay couples with children. Occasionally a humanist wedding is held at the same time.

We find that religious people often comment on how inspiring humanist ceremonies are, and how closely they could relate to all that took place. In other words, while being definitely non-religious, Humanism aims to speak to everyone.

A unique ceremony

Each naming ceremony is unique because there is no set pattern or script that must be followed. This is what so many parents value. You will be able to choose every aspect of the ceremony for yourself, from the statements of commitment to your child's future that you may want to make, to readings, music, or ways of symbolising your welcome. Most ceremonies last about 10 to 15 minutes.

This booklet should give you plenty of ideas! The British Humanist Association's network of celebrants can provide more personal help if you are stuck for ideas.

Where and when?

The most popular place to hold the ceremony is at your home, as part of a celebratory party to welcome your baby. But some people find they have a lot more people they would like to invite than their home can accommodate, and so they decide to hire a room elsewhere.

A naming ceremony can take place on any day of the week, though most often at weekends, and at any sensible time of day. You will probably sense what time of day might be best for your baby, as well as most convenient for your guests. There may be value in waiting until your baby is several months old — well-meaning guests with streaming colds, or long noisy parties, are not the best thing in the world for newly-born babies! And parents may feel too tired from the interrupted nights to have the energy to arrange a party.

Most importantly, when you send out invitations, or ring people up to invite them, make sure you stress that they must be there for a particular start time, so that the ceremony can take place without interruption and with everyone present.

A baby's birth must be registered within a few days at the local Register Office. The BHA does not seek to link that legal requirement with the quite different business of welcoming your child and expressing your love and commitment.

Supporting adults

Since the ceremony is not religious, the phrase 'godparents' is not appropriate. But there is still a useful role that can be played by one or two friends or relatives whom you choose.

What to call them is more difficult. Some people like words such as 'sponsor', 'mentor', 'supporter' or 'special friend'. 'Supporting adult' gives a perfect description, but it's a bit of a mouthful as a phrase. The term 'guardian' sounds good, but do take care, as it has particular legal meaning, and we suggest you avoid using it to describe supporting adults.

The role of a supporting adult is to take a special interest in the child's development and support the parents throughout the long years until the child is an adult, and to be there as a listening ear and welcoming source of advice for the child, outside the immediate family circle.

It can be a great comfort to know that there are people outside your family circle who know your child well and are especially concerned for their welfare and happiness.

For example, lesbian partners bringing up a child together, who have chosen to know and give contact time to the donor-father, may find that appointing him as a supporting adult can be helpful.

Make sure you approach people well in advance of the ceremony if you wish to invite them to be a supporting adult, so that they have time to consider the responsibility carefully.

A framework for the ceremony

Most naming ceremonies have a similar structure, but some are much more elaborate and longer than others. It is usual to have the ceremony at the start of a celebratory party.

Some parts are obvious. There needs to be an opening welcome, a few words about why you have chosen this ceremony and why these particular people have been invited, the actual moment of naming and showing your commitment, and a way of rounding off the ceremony to a suitable celebratory ending.

In some cases, where the child is older, it is perfectly sensible to focus on the welcoming ceremony, and not include a formal naming — everyone present, including perhaps the child, will be very familiar with the name already.

Other elements might be additional readings, music, and involvement of other friends or family members — including any supporting adults.

In this booklet we give suggestions for each of these parts, which you can either borrow for your own ceremony, or use them as inspiration for your own compositions.

Then at the end we give two sample ceremonies in full, to show how everything can fit together.

Who should lead the ceremony?

Some parents can immediately think of a relative or friend who enjoys public speaking, and can stage manage the occasion. Of course, compared with a wedding, this type of ceremony is much more informal, and doesn't need to be quite so carefully planned. Sometimes a parent will take the lead role themselves.

Very often, though, a family will come to the British Humanist Association to be put in touch with a celebrant in their area. Not only can this person help sort out the script and other elements, but they can lead the ceremony on the day, and add a real sense of occasion.

Whatever you decide, it is best if you have a script fully written out, with any readings copied out into it. This means that all you will need is in one place, and is much easier to follow. A well-presented copy of the script, placed in an album with photographs of the ceremony and party, makes a wonderful memento that you can share with your child when they are older.

Examples and Ideas

In this booklet we use the first person singular "I" in all the examples where a participant is speaking. The "we" form can obviously be substituted where two people are speaking together.

"[parent/s]" stands for the name of the parent or parents. The babies will be given different names throughout the booklet.

Introducing the ceremony

The person who is leading the ceremony should call the gathering to order, welcome everyone, and then open the ceremony with a formal introduction. You may like to have a short piece of music played between the welcome and this introduction, especially if guests are to be seated, to give them time to settle down.

The sort of words that have been used include the following examples.

For a short ceremony, the introduction gets straight down to business:

"[Parent/s], you have brought Nicholas here to be welcomed by your family and friends, to name him formally and to appoint supporting adults."

For a longer ceremony, the introduction might be more involved:

"Friends, we have been invited today by [parent/s] for a ceremony to welcome Amy and to celebrate her arrival among us. For many thousands of years people have celebrated the special moments in their lives, with ceremony and ritual, with

feasting, music and dance. There has always been a combination of great seriousness and joy.

"This is a humanist naming ceremony and above all it is an expression of joy. But it is also a time to consider our responsibilities towards Amy and all the children among us. And as we formally name Amy we will mark her individuality and uniqueness as a person, and we will give her that significance even now when she is tiny and helpless."

Another example, from a longer ceremony, for a couple who had also had a humanist wedding:

"I'm delighted to be here today to celebrate Alex's arrival. Two years ago, on a winter's evening, Vicky and Antony celebrated their marriage and made a commitment to love, honour and respect each other. That ceremony marked an important development in their life together, but this ceremony today marks an even more important event because they are now responsible for someone who would not be here, but for them. Today Alex's parents and guardians will share with you their hopes for her future. They are committed to ensuring she has the best possible start in life.

"Vicky and Antony have chosen this non-religious humanist ceremony because they believe that Alex should be free to make her own choices about what she believes when she's older.

"Alex is now 5 months old, so she's had plenty of time to get used to the name she'll be given today.

"For Vicky and Antony, parenthood is a new, exciting and rather daunting responsibility. They've told me they sometimes can't quite believe they <u>are</u> parents. It all takes a lot of getting used to. Parenthood can be both exhilarating and exhausting. You may be head over heels in love with this

small person, but there are times when she's horribly messy, inconveniently demanding, and very noisy — and this is just the beginning. Life will <u>never</u> be the same again.

"Alex has brought Vicky and Antony great joy, and made them both look afresh at what's really important in life. She's given them the opportunity to view the world through a child's eyes once more."

Some adoptive parents wrote these words for their celebrant to say at the start of the ceremony:

"[Parent/s], you have come to us today with your newly adopted child, Ben. After much waiting and much thought, you have been able to welcome a child into your home. You have chosen this child, and he has been chosen for you."

A popular wording includes this:

"All of us here have a special interest in Rachel's welfare and in your happiness together. And today we are formally marking the moment when your partnership becomes a family."

Responsibilities and aspirations for your child

Perhaps the most important part of the ceremony is where you recognise and express your love and commitment to your child, and all the responsibilities that brings with it. You might also express your hopes for your child's future character and life.

Two humanist parents wrote this list of how they saw their commitment. They resolved:

• to take joint responsibility for the welfare of their child;

- to provide continuing love and support, and help their child grow to independence;
- to respect their child as an individual;
- to help their child develop physically and intellectually, by encouragement rather than pressure;
- to influence their child's behaviour by good example, rather than by authoritative orders;
- to help their child to develop her own opinions, beliefs and values.

Here are some other examples of how parents have worded their commitment. As with other anthologies of ideas in this booklet, you can pick and mix the examples that appeal most to you, adding your own ideas as well. These examples may well make you think hard about what you really want for your child's future, and so let you capture those hopes in your words.

"As members and friend's of John's family, we all have a part to play in his growth and development, in his happiness and welfare. Let us each accept our share of responsibility and, through our relationship with John, provide the respect, warmth, honesty and love that he will need."

"We promise to use all our wisdom, patience and love to help Sarah fulfil herself and help others throughout her life."

"Carl, may you learn to love truth, even when it goes against you. May you cultivate kindness. May you find courage, and discover that you are stronger than the things you are afraid of. May you be brave in your own life, and brave in speaking out for justice, and in standing up for what is right. May you have courage to remain loyal to your deep convictions, and courage to admit when you have made a mistake."

"We are mindful that within each child there exists an immense potential that emerges as the years go by — and we realise that the quality of our lives will determine how well this potential is realised. On this day of great promise and joy, we dedicate ourselves to you, Nasrin, and undertake to do our best for you as you grow."

"Bringing a new life into this world is one of the most important things I can do, and it puts a big responsibility on my shoulders. For many years, Ewan will depend on me. The way I look after him, care for and love him, will all play a part in how he grows up, and how his life will be shaped in future years. I promise to do all I can to secure his happiness and strength."

"Without wishing to pre-determine the course of Vanessa's life, or impose upon her our values and expectations, we seek to provide her with an environment in which she is encouraged to develop an open-minded, sensitive and enlightened attitude to life and all those around her."

"Connor, may you have joy in listening and joy in speaking; joy in hearing and joy in seeing; joy in thinking and joy in learning. May your hours be forever bright in play and work, and in friendship and in love."

"May Danielle's life be rich in vision, full in accomplishment, and rejoicing with the ideals of truth and goodness and love."

"Dean, as your parents, we will strive to provide you with a loving and caring home, allow you the freedom to develop your own personality, and endeavour to give you a strong sense of identity and self-esteem.

"We hope to teach you the value of kindness, tolerance and honesty, and hope you will come to love us not only as parents but as friends."

The formal naming

Even though these ceremonies are known as namings, this part is sometimes left out. That is usually because the baby is several months old by the time of the ceremony, and everyone is used to his or her name. But many people find this part is symbolic of their child's unique identity among their family and friends.

At this point in the ceremony, some people like to reinforce that symbolism using flowers, candles, or other ideas. This is dealt with in a later section of this booklet.

At some naming ceremonies everyone present has joined in the formal naming of the child, by repeating after the celebrant similar words to:

"We name this child..."
"...Diana Alison Roberts..."
"...and welcome her into our lives."

This is immediately followed by spontaneous applause and is a very good opportunity for a toast.

Here are some examples of the words used for the formal naming:

"Personal names are part of our uniqueness, part of the personal mystery of the known and unknown in each of us. Our names belong to the core of our private being. Friends have access to our names; strangers do not. Together among friends today, we name this child Ian Jeffrey [+ surname]."

"Sharon Jessica Emma, we are here to bid you welcome and to introduce you to your friends. Although your blood relations are few, your friends are already many, and you are part of the wider world of humanity. I ask all present to witness the giving of your name, and to celebrate our joy in welcoming you."

"And so let us come to the significance of the actual naming. Leo's name will be part of his perception of who he is. It stands for his individuality and his uniqueness. It marks him off from other people, yet brings him to them when they speak his name. So let us share in the joy of this occasion, and name this child Leonardo Grant [+surname]."

"The full name I have given my daughter is Charlotte Beatrice Jane. You may have wondered why I have chosen these names. I chose Charlotte as this was my mother's mother's name; Beatrice I chose as a name that I love; and Jane is my sister's name."

Appointing supporting adults

There are many ways in which you can introduce the idea of supporting adults (humanist equivalent to godparents), and they may wish to join in by saying how they will be there for your child as he or she grows up.

This may be a point when you want to add a symbolic way to mark their appointment, such as through lighting candles, or presenting flowers. More ideas on this are given in a later section.

We give here a selection of words that various people have used relating to supporting adults. The people you choose for this role may well be keen to help write this section.

"Although most of us lead uneventful lives, problems, accidents and illness can and do occur. It is then a great comfort to know that there are others outside the family circle who have a special concern for their child's welfare and happiness. We call these special family friends 'supporting adults'. They are prepared to express their love and concern by making a commitment now to be there for Rory at any future time, to listen, and to give help and support when he needs it."

"[To the supporting adults:] Do you accept a special commitment to Siobhan, to offer friendship and sanctuary, so that she can turn to you in times of doubt or difficulty, with confidence and trust?"

Involving more people in the ceremony

If you have older children or step-children, it is a good idea to give them a practical role in the ceremony. If they are old enough, perhaps they could read a short poem, or play a piece of music. They will appreciate being the centre of attention for part of the ceremony.

If they are younger, you might wish to reaffirm your love and commitment to them, after or as part of your words about your new baby.

Special ways of marking the occasion

These ideas are very personal. Some people choose to add symbolic acts to the ceremony, from lighting candles to planting a tree, while others find them unnecessary. But here are some ideas taken from various ceremonies:

"In this ceremony we give William a flower. It symbolises the beauty and wonder of life, and the meaning of your dedication. Whether a flower comes into full bloom or not, whether it grows tall and strong, whether its purpose is fulfilled, depends on the nurture it receives. No flower grows alone, apart from the sunshine and the rain, apart from the soil from which it grows. So, too, no child grows up alone, and you are here for William, in all the seasons and the times of his days."

"A candle symbolises the potential for creativity and enhancement, warmth and enlightenment, found in each and every child. I light this candle for my daughter, Kelly, to symbolise my dedication to her and her future life."

At the end of the ceremony (and before any party begins!) you might like to provide a book for everyone present to sign, and perhaps write a short message wishing your child well. Like the album with photographs and the script of the ceremony, this makes a wonderful memento.

Ideas for poetry and prose readings

This anthology contains some of the readings that people have found to express their joy, their love, and their commitment. We welcome other ideas too, so please do send us your favourite pieces for possible inclusion in future editions of this booklet.

You may find useful published anthologies in your local library — but be warned, there are many more collections about love and marriage, than there are about small children!

I have no name:
I am but two days old.
What shall I call thee?
I happy am,
Joy is my name.
Sweet joy befall thee!

Pretty joy!
Sweet joy but two days old,
Sweet Joy I call thee:
Thou dost smile,
I sing the while,
Sweet joy befall thee!

Infant Joy** —**William Blake

May she be granted beauty and yet not
Beauty to make a stranger's eye distraught,
Or hers before a looking-glass, for such,
Being made beautiful overmuch,
Consider beauty a sufficient end,
Lose natural kindness and maybe
The heart-revealing intimacy
That chooses right, and never find a friend.

May she become a flourishing, hidden tree,
That all her thoughts may like the linnet be,
And have no business but dispensing round
Their magnanimities of sound,
Nor but in merriment begin a chase,
Nor but in merriment a quarrel.
O may she live like some green laurel
Rooted in one dear perpetual place.

Extract from 'A Prayer For My Daughter' — W B Yeats

My heart leaps up when I behold
A rainbow in the sky;
So was it when my life began;
So be it when I am a man;
So be it when I shall grow old,
Or let me die!
The Child is father of the Man
And I could wish my days to be
Bound each to each by natural piety.

My Heart Leaps Up — William Wordsworth

And now may our hearts be open to all the children of the generations of man, that a circle of love and peace may grow forevermore.

Anon.

Dark brown is the river,
Golden is the sand.
It flows along for ever,
With trees on either hand.

Green leaves a-floating,
Castles of the foam,
Boats of mine a-boating —
Where will all come home?

On goes the river
And out past the mill,
Away down the valley,
Away down the hill.

Away down the river,
A hundred miles or more,
Other little children
Shall bring my boats ashore.

The Child at Play — R L Stevenson

I want to give you something, my child,
for we are drifting in the stream of the world.

Our lives will be carried apart, and our love forgotten.

But I am not so foolish as to hope that I could buy your
heart with my gifts.

Young is your life, your path long, and you drink the
love we bring you at one draught and turn and run away
from us.

You have your play and your playmates. What harm is
there if you have no time or thought for us?

We, indeed, have leisure enough in old age to count the
days that are past, to cherish in our hearts what our
hands have lost for ever.

The river runs swift with a song, breaking through all
barriers. But the mountain stays and remembers, and
follows her with his love.

The Gift — Rabindranath Tagore

On the seashore of endless worlds children meet.

The infinite sky is motionless overhead and the restless water is boisterous. On the seashore of endless worlds the children meet with shouts and dances.

They build their houses with sand, and they play with empty shells. With withered leaves they weave their boats and smilingly float them on the vast deep. Children have their play on the seashore of worlds.

They know not how to swim, they know not how to cast nets. Pearl-fishers dive for pearls, merchants sail in their ships, while children gather pebbles and scatter them again. They seek not for hidden treasures, they know not how to cast nets.

The sea surges up with laughter, and pale gleams the smile of the sea-beach... On the seashore of endless worlds is the great meeting of children.

On the Seashore — Rabindranath Tagore

I have seen a mother at a cot — so I know what love is;

I have looked into the eyes of a child — so I know what faith is;

I have seen a rainbow — so I know what beauty is;

I have felt the pounding of the sea — so I know what power is;

I have planted a tree — so I know what hope is;

I have heard a wild bird sing — so I know what freedom is;

I have seen a chrysalis burst into life — so I know what mystery is;

I have lost a friend — so I know what sorrow is;

I have seen a star-decked sky — so I know what infinity is;

I have seen and felt all these things — so I know what life is.

Anon.

Only recently is it becoming generally recognised that the role of the parent in relation to the upbringing of a child is perhaps the most important thing that happens in our culture. Also, it is being recognised that much has been learned about the process of development during the first five or six years of life. But very little of that knowledge is yet implemented. It should be obvious, then, that our responsibility now is to help our children learn things and learn in ways that were not available to us when we were children. If they are going to make the kind of world in which security can be found, they will have to develop free of many limitations that still bind us.

Yet many people who themselves have developed away from the "certainties" — religious or otherwise — inculcated in them in their childhood, send their children back, by their own teaching or by that of others, to learn things in terms which they themselves have discarded.

This is unfair to children. Surely one's children should be given the advantages of one's own development. Surely they should not be tied hand and foot all over again as their parents were tied to the absolutes of the past generation. Millions of children in the world are now being tied to the certainties of ten and twenty and thirty generations ago by this mechanism, wherein each generation refuses to let its children continue from the point it itself has reached.

The role of a parent — Brock Chisholm

No one is born a new being. He bears in his psyche the imprint of past generations. He is a combination of ancestral units from which a new being must be fused, yet he also bears within him an essential germ, a potential of a unique individual value. The discovery of this unique essence and its development is the quest of consciousness.

What we are — Frances G Wickes

Now this is the day.
Our child,
Into the daylight
You will go out standing.
Preparing for your day.

Our child, it is your day,
This day.
May your road be fulfilled.
In your thoughts may we live,
May we be the ones whom your thoughts will embrace,
May you help us all to finish our roads.

From the writings of the Zuni Indians

humanist baby namings

What have I got exactly? And what am I going to do with her? And what for that matter will she do with me? I have got a daughter, whose life is already separate from mine, whose will already follows its own directions, and who has quickly corrected my woolly preconceptions of her by being something remorselessly different. She is the child of herself and will be what she is. I am merely the keeper of her temporary helplessness. Even so, with luck, she can alter me; indeed, is doing so now. At this stage in my life she will give me more than she gets, and may even later become my keeper. But if I could teach her anything at all — by unloading upon her some of the ill-tied parcels of my years — I'd like it to be acceptance and a relish for life.

What I want for my child is an important beginning, a background where she can most naturally grow. My own background was rough, but it was a good time too, and I want her to have one like it. I was lucky to be raised in a country district, rich with unpackaged and unpriced rewards; and although we were materially poor I believe there are worse things than that kind of poverty. So I would like to give my child chances to be surprised, periods of waiting to sharpen her longings, then some treat or treasure that was worth looking forward to, and an interval to enjoy and remember it.

Given this world to be in, where she can grow reasonably wild, she will also expect the comfort of some authority. To load any child with absolute freedom is to force it to inhabit a wasteland, where it must push its will to find the limits allowed it and grow frantic unless it does. Let her have the assurance, then, of a proper authority, and of a not too inflexible routine, within whose restraints she may take occasional refuge — otherwise I hope she'll be free. I want her to be free from fear to enquire and get answers, free to imagine and tell tall tales, free to be curious and to show enthusiasm, and free at times to invade my silences.

Extracts from 'The Firstborn' — Laurie Lee

Tightly-folded bud,
I have wished you something
None of the others would:
Not the usual stuff
About being beautiful,
Or running off a spring
Of innocence and love —
They will all wish you that,
And should it prove possible,
Well, you're a lucky girl.

But if it shouldn't, then
May you be ordinary;
Have, like other women,
An average of talents:
Not ugly, not good-looking,
Nothing uncustomary
To pull you off your balance,
That, unworkable itself,
Stops all the rest from working.
In fact, may you be dull —
If that is what a skilled,
Vigilant, flexible,
Unemphasised, enthralled
Catching of happiness is called.

Born Yesterday — Philip Larkin

See this small one, tiptoe on
The green foothills of the years,
Views a younger world than yours;
When you go down, he'll be the tall one.

Dawn's dew is on his tongue —
No word for what's behind the sky,
Naming all that meets the eye,
Pleased with sunlight over a lawn.

Hear his laughter. He can't contain
The exquisite moment overflowing.
Limbs leaping, woodpecker flying
Are for him and not hereafter.

Tongue trips, recovers, triumphs,
Turning all ways to express
What the forward eye can guess
That time is his and earth young.

We are growing too like trees
To give the rising wind a voice:
Eagles shall build upon our verse,
Our winged seeds are tomorrow's sowing.

Yes, we learn to speak for all
Whose hearts here are not at home,
All who march to a better time
And breed the world for which they burn.

Though we fall once, though we often,
Though we fall to rise not again,
From our horizon sons begin;
When we go down, they will be tall ones.

Learning to Talk — C Day Lewis

When in the sun the red hot acres smoulder,
Down where the sweating gang its labour plies,
A girl flings down her hoe, and from her shoulder
Unslings her child tormented by the flies.

She takes him to a ring of shadow pooled
By thorn-trees: purpled with the blood of ticks,
While her sharp nails, in slow caresses ruled,
Prowl through his hair with sharp electric clicks.

His sleepy mouth plugged by the heavy nipple,
Tugs like a puppy, grunting as he feeds:
Through his frail nerves her own deep languors ripple
Like a broad river sighing through its reeds.

Yet in that drowsy stream his flesh imbibes
An old unquenched unsmotherable heat
The curbed ferocity of beaten tribes,
The sullen dignity of their defeat.

Her body looms above him like a hill
Within whose shade a village lies at rest,
Or the first cloud so terrible and still
That bears the coming harvest in its breast.

The Zulu Girl — Roy Campbell

A child is the only point on which there converges from
everyone a feeling of love and gentleness. People's souls soften
and sweeten when one speaks of children. The whole of
mankind shares in the deep emotions which they awaken. The
child is a well-spring of love.

Maria Montessori

If a child lives with tolerance,
  she learns to be patient;
If a child lives with encouragement,
  she learns confidence;
If a child lives with praise,
  she learns to appreciate;
If a child lives with fairness,
  she learns judgement;
If a child lives with acceptance and friendship,
  she learns to give love to the world.

adapted from Dorothy Law Nolte

Father: We promise to love and support you
Mother: To be there for you
Father: To listen to you and respect you
Mother: To cherish and guide you
Father: To help you learn right from wrong
Mother: To show you how to respect others and the world around you
Father: To be there whenever you need us
Mother: And to give you our love and make you part of our lives.

Words written by John and Hazel to welcome their daughter Jessica

humanist baby namings

This is the day you will never forget,
It's your red letter day;
We want to make it the happiest yet,
so we're coming to say:

We think it's great you're alive on this earth,
we celebrate your arrival at birth;
If you'll allow us, we'll join in your mirth,
It's your birthday, anything goes!

You've been around a whole year on the ground,
You've been sailing in space;
You've just done a fresh tour of the sun,
with such effortless grace:

Before the next orbit we bring you good cheer,
hope you'll absorb it and keep it all year;
Laugh with your friends, hope the sun never ends,
It's your birthday, anything goes!

This is the day when you first took a bow,
the day you came onto the stage;
The show is still running and you're still a wow,
baby you're all the rage!

No one can tell just how it will go,
but we know well you're the star of the show,
you life's the story let's start a new page,
It's your birthday, anything goes!

*It's your birthday — **John Maguire***

humanist baby namings

Pick me out an old time song
Sing it right or sing it wrong
Play a tune that's nine months long
Welcome to the world.
Take my fiddle and my bow
Play you any tune I know
Keep you dancing while you grow
Welcome to the world.

You've got nappies by the pail
Mum's as skinny as a rail
Got the whole world by the tail
Welcome to the world.
Listen to that baby brawl
You know she thinks she's ten feet tall
And you'd think she'd done it all
Welcome to the world.

In my mind I see you clear
Changing with each day and year
My, we're glad you're finally here
Welcome to the world.
May you grow up proud and strong
May your life be rich and long
May your nights be filled with song
Welcome to the world.

Adapted from a song — Si Kahn

Where am I going? I don't quite know.
Down to the stream where the kingcups grow —
Up to the hill where the pine-trees blow —
Anywhere, anywhere. *I* don't know.

Where am I going? The clouds sail by,
Little ones, baby ones, over the sky.
Where am I going? The shadows pass,
Little ones, baby ones, over the grass.

If you were a cloud and sailed up there,
You'd sail on water as blue as air,
And you'd see me here in the fields and say:
"Doesn't the sky look green today?"

Where am I going? The high rooks call:
"It's awful fun to be born at all."
Where am I going? The ring doves coo:
"We do have beautiful things to do."

If you were a bird, and lived on high,
You'd lean on the wind when the wind came by,
You'd say to the wind when it took you away:
"*That's* where I wanted to go today!"

Where am I going? I don't quite know.
What does it matter where people go?
Down to the wood where the bluebells grow —
Anywhere, anywhere. *I* don't know.

Spring Morning — A A Milne

Sometimes I just hate being small,
When everybody else is tall,
I think the world is most unfair
With me down here and them up there.

It's awful when a juicy peach
Is in a bowl far out of reach
Or parents have safely put away
The toys with which I want to play.

It's terrible to have to stretch
For everything you want to fetch
While bigger people help themselves
To things from off the highest shelves.

Perhaps it might be less unfair
If they were kind of stuck up there
And had to wait till I came round
To give them things from off the ground;

But no, they can easily bend,
To fetch and carry, make and mend,
While if I want to reach that cup,
I have no way of bending up!

Being Small — John Maguire

Using music

It is entirely up to you whether or not you choose to have music during the ceremony. It can add to the sense of occasion, but also has pitfalls.

While communal singing can be inspiring and a good way to involve everyone present, with only a few people there (many of whom may not consider themselves singers!) it can sound a little patchy. If you want everyone to sing, make sure the tune is familiar, and that at least one or two of your guests who enjoy singing have been given a copy in advance so that they are prepared.

Tapes and CDs with short pieces to interweave into the ceremony must be cued up ready, or there will be a messy gap in the proceedings while you find the right track. If you are using recorded music, put someone in charge of it, so that you don't have to worry about too many different things during the ceremony. If you are lucky, you may even find an appropriate song with your child's name in its title.

Live instrumental performances can be wonderful, especially if there are other children involved who can play an instrument.

People have included pieces of music ranging from short classical pieces through to songs currently in the charts. The main thing is that it means something to you.

Two examples of complete ceremonies

THE NAMING CEREMONY
OF GARY ROBSON KERR
Born 11 September 1996
AND HANNAH MARY KERR
Born 11 November 1998

Celebrant: Good afternoon! I am Carole Mountain, invited as a celebrant from the British Humanist Association to lead this ceremony today.

Can I welcome you all here on this special occasion which is to celebrate the birth and naming of these two small children, a son born on 11 September 1996 and a daughter born on 11 November last year. Their parents, Emma and Steven, wish to declare before you the joy that the arival of their children has brought them. This joy is shared by both family and friends — those of you here today, and those who are unable to attend.

Some members of the family are very important to a child, and I would particularly like to mention the children's grandparents, Emma's mother and father, Kath and Jim, and Steven's parents, Mary and Brian. And then two very special people, the greatgrandmothers. Nanna Joan is unable to be here today, but Nanna Irene, we welcome you here.

To all of you, both grandparents and great-grandparents, you will live on in these two small children, as they will have inherited many of your gifts and maybe even much of your personality.

Emma and Steven have brought their children here today to name them formally, and to welcome them, and to celebrate their lives.

Emma and Steven, what names have you chosen for your children?

Emma and Steven: Gary Robson, and Hannah Mary.

Celebrant: Will you do all you can to help them become responsible, self-reliant and caring people, and will you love and cherish their uniqueness and help them develop in every way?

Emma and Steven: We will.

Celebrant: Emma and Steven have asked Emma's sister Jane and her husband Paul to act as special friends for the children. Their role is to look after Gary and Hannah should there be any reason why Emma and Steven are ever unable to do so, and to be there as special friends as they grow up.

Jane and Paul, will you, as best you can, take care of Gary and Hannah, protecting them from harm, listening to them, encouraging and supporting them?

Jane and Paul: We will.

Celebrant: In honour of Gary and Hannah, Emma and Steven will now light two candles. The light stands for these two new lives and the hopes we have for them both. The warmth of the flames represents the warmth of our love and friendship.

[Emma and Steven light the candle.]

Celebrant: Gary Robson Kerr and Hannah Mary Kerr, on behalf of us all here, we welcome you with love.

THE NAMING CEREMONY
OF PATRICK KEVIN WATTS
Born 21 August 1998

Celebrant: Good morning. I am Margaret Nelson, invited as a celebrant from the British Humanist Association to lead this ceremony today.

I'm delighted to welcome you here today to celebrate Patrick's arrival. Helen has chosen this non-religious humanist ceremony because she believes Patrick should be free to make his own choices about what he believes when he is older.

Patrick is now six months old, so he's had plenty of time to get used to the name that we will give him formally today.

He has brought his mother, Helen, great joy, and made her look afresh at what's really important in life. Helen has that rare chance to look once again at the world through a small child's eyes.

Like Helen, the poet W B Yeats was from Ireland, and Helen's friend Mel will now read from his poem "A Prayer for my Daughter".

Mel: May she be granted beauty and yet not
Beauty to make a stranger's eye distraught,
Or hers before a looking-glass, for such,
Being made beautiful overmuch,
Consider beauty a sufficient end,
Lose natural kindness and maybe
The heart-revealing intimacy
That chooses right, and never find a friend.

May she become a flourishing, hidden tree,
That all her thoughts may like the linnet be,
And have no business but dispensing round
Their magnanimities of sound,
Nor but in merriment begin a chase,
Nor but in merriment a quarrel.
O may she live like some green laurel
Rooted in one dear perpetual place.

Celebrant: Thank you, Mel.

A child is a guest in your house, to be loved and respected, but never possessed. Children are generally ungrateful, until they become parents themselves and realise what you did for them — as my mother told me I would! Children learn by experience and example and it takes a long time to learn enough to equip them for independent life. If a child is fortunate, he will be born into a loving environment with food, shelter, and protection from life's dangers. Parents of all species put their children's welfare first, risk their lives to ensure their children's survival.

Good parenting matters not just for the individual child, but for us all, because happy children may become happy, fulfilled people who'll influence everyone around them for the better.

Good parenting is all about balance; between firmness and fairness; between risk and safety. The world is a dangerous place but a child must learn this is so. The Swedish writer Ellen Key wrote, "At every step the child should meet the real experiences of life; the thorns should never be plucked from the roses."

Let us hope that Patrick may trust in the essential goodness of those around him, and avoid being overwhelmed by the harsher aspects of life until he is ready to face them; that he'll develop the unswerving confidence of someone who's never had reason to doubt his worth, because he's been cherished; that he'll develop resilience in greater measure than the portion children are naturally endowed with; that he'll be loved in the future because he has learned to love from those who love him now.

We now come to the most important part of today's ceremony, when Helen states her commitment to Patrick's future.

Helen: Patrick, as your mother, I will strive to provide you with a loving and caring home, allow you the freedom to develop your own personality, and endeavour to give you a strong sense of identity and self-esteem.

I hope to teach you the value of kindness, tolerance and honesty, and hope you will come to love me not only as a mother but as a friend.

May you learn to love truth, even when it goes against you. May you find courage, and discover that you are stronger than the things you're afraid of. May you condemn injustice and stand up for all that is good. May you have the courage to remain loyal to a deep conviction, and the courage to admit when you are wrong.

Celebrant: Helen has chosen her friends Dion, Mel and Tariq to be Patrick's mentors. They will provide Patrick with support, advice and friendship as he grows up.

Dion, Mel and Tariq, do you formally accept a commitment to this child, to offer friendship and sanctuary, so that he can turn to you in times of doubt or difficulty with confidence and trust?

Dion, Mel and Tariq: We do.

Celebrant: Will you all now join with me in saying the words, adapted from Dorothy Law Nolte, which begin, "If a child lives with tolerance"?

All: If a child lives with tolerance,
                    he learns to be patient;
            If a child lives with encouragement,
                    he learns confidence;
            If a child lives with praise,
                    he learns to appreciate;
            If a child lives with fairness,
                    he learns judgement;
            If a child lives with acceptance and friendship,
                    he learns to give love to the world.

Celebrant: Thank you.

A name, once given, will be associated forever with a face, a voice, a walk, a laugh, and all the other idiosyncracies our family and friends recognise. This child's name will be spoken, whispered, shouted, cried, sung, and written — thousands of times, impersonally or meaningfully — by family, friends, neighbours, schoolfellows, teachers, doctors, colleagues, lovers, strangers, and maybe by children and grandchildren. It will define his identity.

[To Patrick] Your name is Patrick Kevin Watts, and we wish you happiness and fulfilment in your life.

[To all] Please raise your glasses to Patrick, and to his future happiness and well-being!

All: To Patrick!

Celebrant: Will you all please sign the special commemorative book with your good wishes for Patrick.

About the BHA

Humanism is an approach to life based on reason and our common humanity, recognizing that moral values are properly founded on human nature and experience alone.

The British Humanist Association is a charity which provides non-religious namings, weddings and funerals, and information on moral issues for schools and colleges. We work to make Religious Education more inclusive, to inform the public about reasoned approaches to ethical questions, and we campaign for a fairer, more rational country for us all to live in.

The BHA has four thousand members, many of whom have joined after attending a ceremony. We would love to welcome you as a member too — please contact the BHA for a free information pack.

Further reading

The BHA publishes a range of booklets and information sheets. Please contact us for a full list. You may be especially interested in Jane Wynne Willson's book *Parenting without God* (available through the BHA) which describes her experiences as a humanist mother. Jane has also written two other guides to ceremonies published by the BHA: *Sharing the Future* about weddings and affirmations, and *Funerals without God*.

If you have children who are at school, or you are choosing a school, the BHA's list of educational resources may be of especial interest to you.

Acknowledgements

The authors would like particularly to thank the following celebrants: Margaret Nelson, Christine Butterworth and Carole Mountain. The BHA is grateful to the publishers who have kindly let us quote from poetry and prose: the Hogarth Press for permission to reproduce a short extract from 'The Firstborn' by Laurie Lee; to Faber and Faber Ltd. for permission to include 'Born Yesterday' by Philip Larkin, from 'The Less Deceived'; to The Peters, Fraser and Dunlop Group Ltd. for permission to reproduce 'Learning to Talk' from The Complete Works of C. Day Lewis, published by Sinclair-Stevenson Ltd.; to Adriaan Donker Ltd. of Johannesburg for permission to include 'The Zulu Girl' by Roy Campbell; to John Maguire; and to Joe Hill Music for permission to quote the song by Si Kahn. Particular acknowledgement is made to the Unitarian Universalist Association of Boston for material found in their collection of readings, 'Great Occasions'.

Above all, we thank all those families whose ideas for naming ceremonies have shaped this book, and we wish them and their children every happiness.